A Different Kind of Christmas
Devotions for the Season

A DIFFERENT KIND OF CHRISTMAS: LIVING AND GIVING LIKE JESUS

An Advent Program by Mike Slaughter

Book: Christmas Is Not Your Birthday

In five short, engaging chapters, readers are inspired to approach Christmas differently and to be transformed in the process.
978-1-4267-2735-1

DVD With Leader Guide

Video programs about ten to fifteen minutes each to accompany and complement the book, one video for each of the five chapters. Leader guide contains everything a leader needs to organize and run a five-session Advent study based on the book and videos, including discussion questions, activities, and flexible session lengths and formats.
978-1-4267-5354-1

Devotional Book: Devotions for the Season

Five weeks of devotional readings for program participants. Each reading includes Scripture, a brief story or meditation, and a prayer.
978-1-4267-5360-2

Youth Study Edition

A five-session Advent study for youth in support of the program. Written in a style and approach to inspire youth. Includes leader helps.
978-1-4267-5361-9

Children's Leader Guide

Complete lesson plans for a five-session Advent study for younger and older children, including activities and handouts.
978-1-4267-5362-6

Mike Slaughter

A Different Kind of Christmas

Devotions for the Season

Abingdon Press
Nashville

A DIFFERENT KIND OF CHRISTMAS:
DEVOTIONS FOR THE SEASON

by Mike Slaughter

Copyright © 2012 by Abingdon Press
All rights reserved.

This book is printed on acid-free, elemental chlorine-free paper.

Scripture quotations marked CEB are from the Common English Bible, © Copyright 2010 by Common English Bible, and are used by permission.

Scripture quotations marked NKJV are taken from the New King James Version®. Copyright © 1982 by Thomas Nelson, Inc. Used by permission. All rights reserved.

Scripture quotations marked NIV are taken from the Holy Bible, New International Version®, NIV®. Copyright © 1973, 1978, 1984, 2011 by Biblica, Inc.™ Used by permission of Zondervan. All rights reserved worldwide. www.zondervan.com. The "NIV" and "New International Version" are trademarks registered in the United States Patent and Trademark Office by Biblica, Inc.™

Scripture quotations marked NLT are taken from the Holy Bible, New Living Translation, copyright © 1996, 2004, 2007. Used by permission of Tyndale House Publishers, Inc., Carol Stream, Illinois 60188. All rights reserved.

Special thanks to Karen Smith

ISBN 978-1-4267-5360-2

Library of Congress Cataloging-in-Publication applied for.
12 13 14 15 16 17 18 19 20 —10 9 8 7 6 5 4 3 2 1
MANUFACTURED IN THE UNITED STATES OF AMERICA

Contents

Introduction

It was November, and my wife Carolyn and I were at the Tri-County Mall outside Cincinnati. Thanksgiving was still three weeks away, but already the mall was decorated for Christmas, Santa's elves were assembling his throne, and our favorite radio station was playing around-the-clock holiday tunes!

In the midst of the season's noise, it's hard to find the heart of God. Yet if you listen closely, you can hear the words of Jesus:

All I want for Christmas, for my birthday, is for you to remember the poor, reach the lost, and set the oppressed free.

This Advent, I am challenging you to celebrate a different kind of Christmas—a Christmas that cuts through the hype and doesn't leave you exhausted and broke at the end of the year. It will be a Christmas that puts Jesus in his rightful role as the center, founder, and purpose of our celebration.

Over the next five weeks, we will spend time together and with God avoiding the overspending, overeating, over-worrying, and busyness that have become the hallmarks of the holiday season. Instead, we will expect, and become part of, the miracle that Jesus wants to perform this Christmas through you and me—sacrificial actions that can transform lives both far away and close to home, transforming us in the process.

Each week will begin with a brief story about what can happen when you remember that Christmas is not your birthday, that it's Jesus' birthday, and you intentionally focus on honoring him. Then, during the week, you will have a devotional time each day, including Scripture, story, and a prayer. Week by week, you will be encouraged this Advent to

- expect a miracle;
- give up false expectations of the perfect Christmas;
- experience (and demonstrate) God's scandalous love;
- "shop" for Jesus' wish list, not your own;
- commit to taking a different road.

Jesus' birthday will be here soon. Let's start celebrating!

WEEK ONE

Expect a Miracle

I love *The Lord of the Rings* trilogy by J. R. R. Tolkien, a great writer of the mid-twentieth century. The three books are not only exciting adventure stories but also demonstrate what it means to be the people of God. The third book in the trilogy, *The Return of the King,* always reminds me that we are living in that "between" time right now—the time between Jesus' first appearance on Earth and the moment of his return. Sam and Frodo, the two Hobbit heroes of the trilogy, know that they must leave the safe comfort of their Shire to become revolutionaries for good. Against their better judgment and peace-loving, risk-averse nature, they set off for the evil land of Mordor, risking heart, home, and even their lives, to move against the forces of darkness. In one particularly bleak moment deep in the enemy's territory, Sam is able to spot a single star shining out of the darkness above the heavy clouds of Mordor. Sound familiar? "The light shines in the darkness, and the darkness has not overcome it" (John 1:5 NIV). Even in the deepest darkness, the true light has come into the world, and darkness can never eradicate it.

Within the church, especially in the past century, we have reduced Christmas to pageants, presents, candle lighting, and carol singing. We converted Saint Nicholas into Santa Claus, and then rolled them both into our picture of Jesus. We started memorializing the birth of the Savior through comfortable trivialities instead of following him into battle against the kingdom of darkness. We forget, or ignore entirely, that we are to be kingdom operatives, like Sam and Frodo, serving as Christ's revolutionaries of hope in the world.

This week we will remind ourselves that the miracle of Christmas looks nothing like the materialism of our culture. Instead we will learn how to expect the miracle—and be the miracle—until the return of our King and the full restoration of his Kingdom.

1. How Do You Picture God?

*He was despised and avoided by others, a man who suffered,
who knew sickness well. Like someone from whom people hid their
faces, he was despised, and we didn't think about him.*
(Isaiah 53:3 CEB)

*The Lord God's spirit is upon me, because the Lord has
anointed me. He has sent me to bring good news to the poor.*
(Isaiah 61:1 CEB)

How do you picture God? Some of us see God as a harsh, judgmental father, much like our own flawed dad, or as a capricious Zeus hurling thunderbolts from heaven at unsuspecting humans. At Christmas, our picture of God closely aligns with that of our culture, depicting God as "Santa Claus coming to town"—both a watchful stalker who knows when we've been bad or good and rewards or withholds gifts accordingly; and a magical gift-giver who showers us with toys and electronics we don't need, all the while saddling us with more credit card debt (one gift that truly does keep on giving . . . or taking).

Jesus should be our "God with skin on." But, even then, we often mess it up. My childhood picture of Jesus was *The Head of Christ,* by Walter Sallman, the painting that hung in almost every Sunday school class I attended. I'm sure you know it! In the painting, Jesus' face is glowing against a soft brown background as he gazes pensively toward a distant, heavenly horizon. His skin is flawless; his hair is clean and flowing. It's a beautiful painting but doesn't seem to resemble the Messiah from Isaiah 53:2 (CEB): "He possessed no splendid form for us to see, no desirable appearance." In the movie Talladega Nights, racecar driver Ricky Bobby, played by Will Ferrell, addresses all prayers to his own particular picture of Jesus—an eight-pound, six-ounce bouncing baby boy.

Before we can expect the miracle of a different kind of Christmas, first we must work on our image of Immanuel, God With Us. We must recognize in Jesus a God who knows what it means to feel pain, heartbreak, love, and joy. We must see a God who prioritizes the poor, the widowed, and the orphaned, and a Savior who loves us enough not only to die for us but to model for us how to live sacrificially in his name, so that we become co-workers in a Christmas miracle.

Lord God, help me to see your face and feel your hand this Advent season. Let my heart be broken by that which breaks yours. May I be your hands and feet for growing miracles. Amen.

2. THE BEST GIFTS DON'T COME IN STOCKINGS

*Therefore the Lord will give you a sign. The young woman is
pregnant and is about to give birth to a son, and she will name him
Immanuel. (Isaiah 7:14 CEB)*

When we worship a Santa Claus Jesus, we overlook a simple truth: that the best gifts don't come in stockings. We appreciate only those gifts that are adorned with bows, frills, and brightly colored wrapping; and we fail to recognize the good gifts we have already received . . . or those that are about to come.

One of the best gifts I ever received was in June 2007, when I spent Father's Day with my son Jonathan on the ground in Darfur, Sudan, a war zone. We had traveled there to witness God's miracle of saving lives through the sacrificial gifts of our first two Christmas Miracles offerings from Ginghamsburg Church.

Last Christmas, although I loved the new watch from my wife Carolyn, my best gift arrived during Christmas Eve worship when I baptized my newest granddaughter, Anna Claire Leavitt. All grandbabies are precious, but this baptism held special significance, since we had found out a few months before that little Anna had been born with heart issues. We continue to move forward with God, trusting that one day she will be completely healed.

Even these great gifts in my life pale in comparison with the gift of Immanuel, God With Us. Once we grasp the complete significance of that gift, no brightly wrapped shirt, gadget, or game will ever compare, or even matter. Through the power of Immanuel in my own life, I was lost but now am found; I was blind but now I see. I was a D student in high school who played in a band that was busted for drugs, and now I'm an author, a speaker, a pastor with a doctorate, and, along with my church, a world changer.

Once we fully grasp the gift of Immanuel, we are compelled to share Jesus with the world—not as a magical gift giver, but as a miracle worker. Our Messiah didn't shimmy down a chimney but hung on a cross. Now, that's a gift! It's a gift beyond all measure, and we must receive it in our hearts, not in our stockings.

Lord, this Christmas, let me not focus on the materialistic gifts I crave that bring momentary happiness. Help me to recognize the good gifts I already have received, embracing an attitude of gratitude and generosity, celebrating the season with such an infectious spirit that it draws others to you. Amen.

3. PRESENCE—NOT PRESENTS

You cannot serve God and wealth. (Matthew 6:24 CEB)

When we look at our current understanding of Christmas, we can see that we have mixed together some Santa Claus theology, a few Victorian-era practices of the nineteenth century, and a little biblical truth to create a kind of Christianity that's more like Frosty the Snowman than the events of the first Christmas Day. Even our favorite Christmas hymns can paint the wrong picture: "The cattle are lowing, the baby awakes, but little Lord Jesus no crying he makes." That doesn't seem likely! I swear, each of my kids had colic for the first six months.

We have also set unrealistic goals for ourselves, trying to create an ideal, magical Christmas experience that simply is not attainable. Last December I made the mistake of asking a certain woman if she was ready for Christmas. Instead of the usual polite response of "almost," or "getting there," or even "no," she rattled off a "to do" list that left me dizzy—shopping, wrapping, baking, card addressing, party hosting, and concerts that took a good five minutes to describe. Where was Christ on her list?

The only way we will experience a miracle this Christmas, and next, is if we start creating new traditions for ourselves in our homes and churches—traditions that focus on the miracle worker instead of the materialism. Let's start traditions that emphasize one another, rather than the presents we expect to receive and go into debt to purchase. Even more importantly, we need to make space in our schedules and in our hearts for the presence of Jesus—first receiving the miracle, so that we can then be God's conduits for delivering the miracle.

There is a precedent for presents in the biblical Christmas narrative. In Matthew 2, we see the magi arriving with gifts for Jesus of gold, frankincense, and myrrh. So, how should we celebrate the birth of the miracle worker? By giving our presence, our presents, and honoring Jesus on his birthday by sharing our treasures with the least and the lost.

Lord, in the frantic pace of the Advent season, I will focus on your presence—not the presents. I will choose the miracle over the materialism, both receiving it and then sharing it with others. Amen.

4. RÉSUMÉ: MIRACLE WORKER

You will receive power when the Holy Spirit has come upon you, and you will be my witnesses. (Acts 1:8 CEB)

When was the last time you updated your résumé? Most of us are careful to list all the positions we have held (at least those that make us look good) and the critical skills we have developed and utilized to excel in those positions. Well, God invites all his followers—that means you—to add yet another "position held" to your list: miracle worker. In 2 Corinthians 6:1, the apostle Paul describes us as being "co-workers in Christ." Acts 1:8 reminds us that we receive the power of God when the presence of the Holy Spirit invades our lives.

Do you feel that you lack the qualifications to be a miracle worker? The Scripture is full of stories about God using ordinary, unqualified, and even seriously messed up people to accomplish miracles. An inarticulate Moses led God's people out of slavery and into the Promised Land. David, an adulterer and murderer, was described as a man after God's own heart and was the greatest king of the ancient Israelites. Paul, a persecutor of Christians, authored the majority of the New Testament after his encounter with the risen Christ on the road to Damascus. Mary, an unwed teenager from a humble background, gave birth to the Son of God.

We don't lack examples of miracle workers in more contemporary times either. Mother Teresa, a tiny woman from

Albania, became one of the most influential miracle workers of the twentieth century as she humbly served the poor in Calcutta, India. There was nothing of earthly note in her résumé that would have predicted her impact. I barely managed to graduate high school after nearly flunking my junior year. Yet, I have been privileged to pastor a church for thirty-three years that has invested $5.6 million into the Sudan for sustainable humanitarian projects through eight miracle offerings made at Christmas.

God is inviting you to add "miracle worker"—co-worker with Christ—to your résumé. You have been called and equipped. You already have the power to create change in the world through God's action in your life. This Advent, God doesn't need the elaborate, the expensive, or the extraordinary to bring about his miracles. He only needs you.

Lord, thank you for equipping me to be your conduit for serving people this Christmas. I may be an ordinary person, but I recognize that I serve an extraordinary God who will work in me and through me to accomplish miracles. Amen.

5. FINDING MY MIRACLE

The angel said, "Don't be afraid, Mary. God is honoring you.
Look! You will conceive and give birth to a son, and you will name
him Jesus." (Luke 1:30-31 CEB)

This Advent, where is God calling you to be a miracle worker? After all, the world is full of crises. As I write this, the Arab Spring that started in 2011 continues to result in government oppression and violent uprisings in Africa and the Middle East. Closer to home, the effects of the Great Recession that started in 2008 continue to mean high unemployment rates, more kids who go to bed hungry at night, and an ever-increasing gap between the haves and have-nots. Even if you are willing to be a miracle worker for God, how do you know where to begin?

The angel Gabriel gave Mary a vision of what God wanted to do through her. Our challenge is to create a clear picture in our minds of what God wants to accomplish through us. What are you seeing or hearing right now that creates discomfort in your spirit? Whom is God placing in your path? How are you currently serving that gets your heart pumping a little faster every time you think about it? Where do you see God already working?

Years ago, John, a member of Ginghamsburg Church, spent hours enjoyably tinkering around with automobiles. He decided to use that hobby to create a car ministry, making it possible for single moms and those in need to have reliable transportation, a critical part of holding down any job.

A church member who was working at the food pantry heard story after story of elderly clients using their food supplies to take care of beloved four-legged companions. This church member founded our Paws4Hope ministry to meet that unique need.

I'm a car buff, and one Sunday after church I was busy checking out automobile ads, when on the opposite page I noticed a photo of an emaciated child, a victim of the violence in the Sudan. I was struck by the juxtaposition of a Sedan with the Sudan. The former I knew everything about; the latter I knew nothing about. In that moment, God planted in me the seed of our congregation's work in the Sudan.

You, as a spirit-filled Christian, have the potential to have God move within you. You just need to dream God's dream and then act on God's vision.

Lord God, I am listening and watching, ready to have you birth a Christmas miracle through me. I am your servant. Amen.

6. PAYING THE PRICE

The righteousness that I have comes from knowing Christ, the
power of his resurrection, and the participation in his sufferings.
(Philippians 3:10 CEB)

What runs through your mind when you read the Scripture above? To me, "knowing Christ" sounds great. What an honor. And "the power of his resurrection?" I'm all over that. Then I come to "the participation in his sufferings." Whoa! I didn't sign up for suffering, did I? Well, yes, I did. You did too.

For our lives to be meaningful, we need to give them away. A meaningful Christmas won't be found in personal comfort and material luxuries; rather, we will find meaning—we will receive and deliver God's miracle—when we are ready and willing to pay the price. This basic truth is the antithesis of our culture's values. Each week we look forward to TGIF, "thank God it's Friday," when we can exit the workweek. When we hit fifty our mantra becomes "I can't wait until I retire." And at Christmas we emphasize "the holly and the jolly" instead of Jesus.

Even when we do bring Jesus into our Christmas celebrations, we understandably focus on the cradle of the baby Jesus, forgetting that we cannot separate the cradle from the cross. The cross, not the cradle, is the center of the Christian message. When Jesus is teaching the disciples about his impending death in John 12, he says, "I assure you that unless a grain of wheat falls into the earth and dies, it can only be a single seed. But if it dies, it bears much fruit" (John 12:24 CEB). Jesus' resurrection had to be preceded by his crucifixion.

Christmas is about a miracle. But, as Mary discovered, miracles don't just happen; they are born through the pains of labor. Immanuel has come to move us out of our comfort zones so that God may work through us this Advent to make the impossible possible.

Covenant Prayer
From John Wesley's Covenant Service, 1780

I am no longer my own, but thine.
Put me to what thou wilt, rank me with whom thou wilt.
Put me to doing, put me to suffering.
Let me be employed by thee or laid aside for thee,
exalted for thee or brought low for thee.
Let me be full, let me be empty.
Let me have all things, let me have nothing.
I freely and heartily yield all things to thy pleasure and
disposal.
And now, O glorious and blessed God, Father, Son, and
Holy Spirit, thou art mine, and I am thine. So be it.
And the covenant which I have made on earth,
let it be ratified in heaven. Amen.

Giving Up on Perfect

To experience a different kind of Christmas, we have to get beyond our cultural concept of "the perfect Christmas."

I suspect God may have written the original lyrics of that ubiquitous country song from the early 1970s: "I beg your pardon, I never promised you a rose garden."* Actually, if you think about it, God did give us a rose garden, until we allowed sin to trample through it and pull up perfection by the roots. Life is an incredible gift; but, let's face it, life is messy. We aren't perfect people, and we don't lead perfect lives. However, we do have a perfect God, who invites us, in spite of ourselves, to be part of his rebuilding, renewing, and restoring movement on Earth.

I was recently asked to name one of my favorite Christmas memories as an adult. The first one that came to mind was the time I was accosted by the police at Ginghamsburg's youth

* "Rose Garden," 1970, Columbia Records, written by Joe South, recorded by Lynn Anderson.

building early one Christmas morning. Talk about not perfect! At the time, my son Jonathan was a student at the University of Pennsylvania, where he played Division I baseball. He and I had slipped out of the house early that morning to use the batting cage at the church. I am no athlete, but I have always been passionate about baseball, and tossing Jonathan balls as he worked on his swing was a favorite pastime. I had a key to the building but of course had no clue that the security system was engaged (or remembered that we had one, for that matter). The police arrived, and so did our facilities manager, who probably was less than thrilled to be called out so early on Christmas. But, it was a great morning—and a Christmas to remember!

This week we will discover how to experience a different kind of Christmas, by focusing not on perfect presents but on the perfect *presence* of God, and on the people he has given us to love and to serve.

7. REDEFINING PERFECT

While they were there, the time came for Mary to have her
baby. She gave birth to her firstborn child, a son, wrapped him
snugly, and laid him in a manger, because there was no place for
them in the guestroom. (Luke 2:6-7 CEB)

What does your perfect Christmas look like? Having the most brightly lit exterior in the neighborhood, the one that winds up being featured by the weather guy as "house of the day" on the local TV news? Filling kitchen counters with platters of home-baked cookies and candies, or at least good imitations that have been removed from the telltale store-bought packaging? Piling up gifts so high under the tree that your three-year-old could stand behind them and be completely hidden? For some of us, it's all of that . . . and more. We place so many expectations upon the season and ourselves.

Last Christmas, my wife Carolyn wound up setting up the tree by herself. In our crazy Advent schedule, it was the only available night she had, and I was committed to a meeting at church. By the time I got home, Carolyn was frustrated, to say the least. In trying to make the perfect Christmas, she had spent two hours figuring out why the middle section of the tree wouldn't light up. She had checked and rechecked every bulb on a tree that was supposed to work even when a few lights were out. It had lit up just fine when we put it away the year before. Can you relate?

My favorite part of Christmas is the family celebration. After all, we experience God through relationships. I spend each Christmas Day in my own home, after preaching as many as seven times on Christmas Eve. As a result, extended family comes to stay with us. Talk about no room in the inn! People sleep everywhere. Carolyn and I use a blow-up mattress in my study, someone else takes the foldout sofa in the basement, all the couches are full, and I love it.

Preparing for Jesus is a whole lot different from preparing for Christmas. This year, let's not get so caught up in the preparations that we miss the people—or the Messiah. Mary knew how to do it. She simply took the greatest gift the world has ever received, wrapped him snugly in a blanket, and placed him in a manger.

Result? Christ-mass.

Lord, this Advent, empower me to slow down, simplify, and savor—savor the season, and savor the Savior. Amen.

8. A SANITIZED NATIVITY

When Elizabeth was six months pregnant, God sent the angel
Gabriel to Nazareth, a city in Galilee, to a virgin who was engaged
to a man named Joseph, a descendant of David's house. The
virgin's name was Mary. (Luke 1:26-27 CEB)

I love Christmas carols, and one of my favorites is "Away in a Manger." But, talk about a sanitized view of Christmas! It paints a sweet picture of the little Lord Jesus soundly asleep in the hay, while the cattle are "lowing" right next to him. I'll bet lowing wasn't the only thing those cows were doing—they were being cows!

Jesus was born in a barn, placed in an animal food trough, and surrounded by manure. There was nothing clean, neat, or sweet smelling about it. There was also the messy business of Jesus' mother, Mary. Can you imagine what first ran through her mind when Gabriel told her she was about to become an unwed teenage mother—this in a culture that stoned people for less? Joseph didn't have it easy either. I imagine that throughout Jesus' childhood, folks back in Nazareth whispered about Mary's bastard son that Joseph had been cajoled into raising as his own. Jesus' early childhood wasn't much cleaner or more predictable than his birth. King Herod, told about Jesus' birth by the Magi, unleashed a campaign of genocide on male children, forcing Jesus' family to flee on short notice, becoming refugees in Africa.

These days it's easy to sanitize that first Christmas. After all, children born outside of marriage have almost become the norm in some circles, and genocide is something that happens "over there." Also, we've already read the back of the book, so we know the good guy wins. But to Mary and Joseph, all of this had to be scary stuff.

To experience a different kind of Christmas this year, we need to recognize that following Jesus can be messy and inconvenient. Our paths won't always be safe or predictable. Dung happens. We may love those high-flying mountaintop moments, but real growth happens in the well-fertilized valleys (spelled m-a-n-u-r-e).

No matter what mess we find ourselves in this Christmas, whether one of our own making or one God is inviting us to enter, we will remember that God is in it with us, and God will work out his miracles through us.

Lord, help me to give up on perfect this Christmas. Help me to remember that my mess can become your miracle. I am never alone. Amen.

9. A Rescue Mission

*God so loved the world that he gave his only Son, so that
everyone who believes in him won't perish but will have
eternal life. (John 3:16 CEB)*

*Look! I'm standing at the door and knocking. If any hear my
voice and open the door, I will come in to be with them, and will
have dinner with them, and they will have dinner with me.
(Revelation 3:20 CEB)*

What is the real meaning of Christmas? You just read it.

Those two verses (the first of which my grandmother taught
me when I was four) contain the most profound truths you and I
need to know. God came for us, and God is still here with us.
We need to embrace the reality of God's presence, and remember
that he loves us no matter how messed up we are.

rescue, and Christmas is the time to celebrate that mission.

A few years ago, when traveling in Israel with a group of religious leaders and government officials, I was invited by a law
professor to *Shabbat,* the Sabbath meal, one Friday evening.
The professor, an Orthodox Jew, led us through the liturgy of
the *Shabbat*. Afterward he said to me, "I wish we had the
Christian concept of grace. No one else has it, and it's called
forgiveness."

Ultimately, the Christmas message is about God's pursuit of
us and his forgiveness, even when we run away from him.

Giving up on perfect this Christmas means extending grace to ourselves, and to others. This may translate into forgiving the sister-in-law we haven't spoken to for a year because of a dispute over last year's Christmas ham. Or it might mean reaching out to rescue the least and the lost, even when we are convinced they are responsible for their own current mess.

That's the real meaning of Christmas.

Lord, your grace is sufficient for me. May I embrace it for myself and extend it to others this Christmas. Amen.

10. FAVORED, NOT PERFECT

When the angel came to her, he said, "Rejoice, favored one!
The Lord is with you!" She was confused by these words and won-
dered what kind of greeting this might be. The angel said, "Don't
be afraid, Mary. God is honoring you. Look! You will conceive and
give birth to a son, and you will name him Jesus."
(Luke 1:28-31 CEB)

If I had been Mary, I think my response would have been, "Thanks, but no thanks." An unexpected virgin pregnancy was probably not at the top of Mary's life plans. And, this great promised gift of a son would lead, thirty-four years later, to a cross.

Have you ever been doing everything right when wrong shows up? I can think of many examples in my life, ranging from inconveniences to major life issues. I can't tell you how many times Carolyn and I have been blessed with the unexpected appearance of a little extra cash, maybe through an unanticipated refund or some income from a last-minute speaking opportunity, only to have the family car or a major home appliance fail the very next day. Easy come, easy go.

In August 2011, our daughter gave birth to our third beautiful granddaughter. All seemed perfect; we couldn't have been prouder. Weeks later, we were told that the baby had a serious heart condition.

One of our most faithful Ginghamsburg members, Elaine, a retired school principal who staffs our reception desk on weekends and finds a way to serve each time the doors are open, lost her daughter—the mother of two—to a heart attack; Elaine also had serious surgery on her leg and was diagnosed with breast cancer. All of this occured within three years' time. We can be favored of God, and evil still shows up.

The path of faith isn't predictable. Bad things happen to good people. The world itself isn't bad, but it is broken. Whenever I start to feel sorry for myself and my circumstances, I flip over to Hebrews 11 and start reading about the heroes of the faith. Many of them were tortured, killed, even sawn in two. That certainly makes some of my life's challenges seem more manageable.

Part of giving up on perfect this Christmas is recognizing that life, though it isn't perfect, can be perfecting. As the apostle Paul writes in Romans 5:3-4, "We even take pride in our problems, because we know that trouble produces endurance, endurance produces character, and character produces hope." (CEB)

Lord, I confess that I am blessed. Please be in all the painful places of my life this Christmas, and make me present to the pain of others. Amen.

11. PROACTIVE FAITH

*Then Mary said to the angel, "How will this happen since I
haven't had sexual relations with a man?" The angel replied, "The
Holy Spirit will come over you and the power of the Most High will
overshadow you. Therefore, the one who is to be born will be holy.
He will be called God's Son. (Luke 1:34-35 CEB)*

The journey of faith isn't easy. I have been on this journey
since 1969, when I was a freshman in college. For some reason,
doubt has been my constant companion for the forty-plus years
since. It shouldn't be surprising. If you really think about it,
every major decision I have made during that period has been
based on a dead man walking out of a tomb alive—a man who
allegedly was born to a virgin. That's some tough stuff to
believe. In fact, I find myself skeptical when someone says to
me, "Well, I have never had any problems with doubt." It makes
me wonder if they have ever made a real commitment to the
journey of faith.

When Mary received the "good news" from the angel that
she was about to become pregnant, she must have been flabber-
gasted. It's no wonder she asked, "How will this happen?" In
the moments following that conversation, the angel disappeared,
leaving no physical sign that he had ever been there, and Mary
had to choose between two opposing options: the paralysis of
fear and defeat, or proactive faith. It's so amazing to me that,
given her situation, she chose the latter. In fact, she chose it

wholeheartedly, to the point that she was able to proclaim a few verses later in Luke 1:46, "With all my heart I glorify the Lord!"

We see this same proactive faith in Joseph. He found out about Mary's pregnancy and at first sought a quiet divorce. He must have been in deep disillusionment and emotional pain, no doubt feeling betrayed by the person he trusted the most and, quite possibly, by God. He then had his own angelic visit, when God's messenger showed up and Joseph committed to moving forward in faith. Based on Scripture, by the way, it appears that unlike Mary, Joseph never lived to see Jesus turn water into wine, make blind eyes see, or resurrect anyone from the grave. Nevertheless, Joseph was a great earthly father to the Son of God.

We all have struggles. We all have doubts. What matters is how we choose to respond. Joseph and Mary chose to act on God's promise. Will you?

Lord God, I believe; help my unbelief. This Christmas, may I shake off the paralysis of fear and doubt and move forward in proactive faith, living in your promise. Amen.

12. THE GIFT OF SELF

When Elizabeth heard Mary's greeting, the child leaped in her womb and Elizabeth was filled with the Holy Spirit. With a loud voice she blurted out, "God has blessed you above all woman, and he has blessed the child you carry." (Luke 1:41-42 CEB)

When Mary showed up pregnant and unmarried at Elizabeth's doorstop, Elizabeth took her in. She not only provided physically for her young cousin; she also gave Mary encouragement and wisdom from her own experience as Mary prepared to give birth to a miracle. God often places people in our paths who have experienced struggles similar to our own and made it through. Likewise, God can use our pain and eventual hope to provide seeds for miracles in others.

Doug and Deb have been married for thirty years. Doug leads a support group for men struggling with sexual addiction, and Deb mentors women who are in relationship with sexually addicted men. They are one another's best partners and cheerleaders in ministry. What makes them so effective? They have been there, done that. Doug struggled with his own addiction for years, which eventually resulted in an affair. With the help of their faith community and its support systems, they made the challenging journey back to a healthy marriage. God now uses Doug and Deb to give others that same hope.

Alex was sexually abused by his brother as a child. As a young adult, he became addicted to drugs and alcohol. Now in his fifties, he helps to lead our recovery ministry. Alex not only inspires those in recovery who attend our Next Step worship service; he inspires me.

Another recovering addict in our church, Mark, speaks to youth groups and addicts about his journey "from dope to hope." About eight years ago, Mark was diagnosed with a malignant brain tumor. (He's now in remission.) His Jewish neurosurgeon was so inspired by Mark's faith and positive spirit that he decided to attend worship with Mark one weekend—at Christmas! Mark's battle with terminal cancer demonstrated to many what it means to live well and to die with grace. Our best financial counselors are often those who have taken herculean steps to get out of personal debt.

This year, as you give up on creating the perfect party, package, present, or pecan pie, perhaps the best Christmas gift you can give is the gift of yourself. Life gets messy. Use your mess . . . to bless.

Lord, show me this Advent how I can join your mission in healing the souls of the world, knowing that I will find true peace and joy through serving others in Christ's spirit. Amen.

WEEK THREE

Scandalous Love

Christmas is when God shows up in the unexpected to the unaccepted . . . to the fragile, the poor, and the disenfranchised.

When the King of the universe comes to redeem his creation, he chooses the form of a vulnerable baby born to humble parents. His mother, an unwed teen, calls into question the legitimacy of his birth to a skeptical culture. His town of birth, Bethlehem, belongs to one of the least prestigious and least powerful tribes in Israel. His birth is first revealed to "unclean" shepherds, who are alienated from full participation in the religious institutions of their people. God then shares the revelation with the Magi, foreigners from the east who are gentile infidels.

Why does God choose such unlikely ways of revealing himself? He does so to make it perfectly clear, through the miracle of Christmas, that he is willing to risk it all in an urgent attempt to save us all, no exceptions. He is a God of scandalous love.

So, how do we respond to this incredible gift, this crazy excess of love? Matt, a technician on the road from job site to site, stocks his work van with hats and gloves to pass through windows to the homeless. Beth, a young schoolteacher, has used her Christmas break for five straight years to lead Hurricane Katrina rebuilding trips to the Gulf. Dan is working hard for bush pilot certification, ready to fly in supplies and hope in Africa after retirement. Dr. Samuel goes to Jamaica time and time again, a pied piper who recruits medical personnel to provide care to the indigent. Hundreds of Ginghamsburg families intentionally choose to live more simply each Christmas so that others may simply live. These families gave nearly six million in eight miracle offerings to save the lives of people they will never meet. Why? "For the love of Christ compels us" (2 Corinthians 5:14 NKJV).

Your challenge this week is first to accept that scandalous love as your own, and then to live it generously for others.

13. LOVE AFFAIR

*But he emptied himself by taking the form of a slave and by
becoming like human beings. When he found himself in the form of
a human, he humbled himself by becoming obedient to the point of
death, even death on a cross. (Philippians 2:7-8 CEB)*

Tipp City, where I live, holds an annual Christmas festival in its historic district in early December. About seven years ago, I was invited to host a signing of my book *Momentum for Life* at the Hotel Gallery, a restored inn from the 1800s that houses a pottery shop and sells other unique gifts. As I signed, I noticed that one woman in the line kept staring at me. I couldn't place her definitively, but she looked vaguely familiar. When she finally approached the table, I asked if she had attended my alma mater in Cincinnati. She said no, but then blurted out that she had attended a neighboring school and had been my date at a high school Christmas formal—the only dance to which I took an actual date in my entire high school career.

It's funny how memories start flooding in when you reminisce about your days in public school. For a few of us, perhaps those were the glory days and we would gladly go back and relive a few of them. For me, the memories aren't so great. I remember being stood in a trash can during grade school because I had wet my pants; I recall my mom's perpetual dismay at my report cards; and I reluctantly admit to being one of the last guys picked for teams in gym class. Here I was thirty-seven years later, a pastor, an author asked to do a book signing, and yet that brief encounter momentarily took me back to feeling like a skinny, inadequate teenager again.

Many esteem deficiencies that started in our childhood can carry over into our relationship with God. We may believe in God but wonder how God could ever possibly believe in us. We aren't tall, smart, strong, beautiful, productive, or good enough to merit God's love.

Perhaps the best news that Christmas brings to us each year is this: God is absolutely crazy about us, crazy enough to take on human form to pursue us ... and then to hang on a cross for us.

God has a scandalous love affair with humanity—and yes, that includes you.

Lord, this Christmas, help me to see myself through your eyes. Empower me to love myself, so that I may then go and love others in your name. Amen.

14. FATAL DISTRACTIONS

*I am the LORD your God who brought you out of Egypt, out of
the house of slavery. You must have no other gods before me.
(Exodus 20:2-3 CEB)*

Our cultural celebration of Christmas is full of what I call
"fatal distractions," things that shove God from being the front-
and-center priority in our lives onto the back of the shelf—right
behind that big-screen TV that's a steal of a deal at 4 a.m. on
Black Friday. If you think about it, Christmas is the perfect time
to become distracted from God's priorities. The culture says,
"shop 'til you drop," the holiday parties say, "overindulge," and
the Joneses next door challenge you (at least in your mind) to
top the flashy Santa's sleigh that's displayed in their front yard.

Your fatal distractions may not be the same as mine. For in-
stance, money is not a temptation for me, but it might be for
you. You could leave a thousand dollars on the table in front of
me in an otherwise unoccupied room, and I wouldn't be tempted
to touch it. But Christmas can really appeal to one of my
greatest temptation: materialism. I can't wait to get each new
iGadget that comes out, am picky about where I purchase my
clothes, and have been known in days past to purchase an
exclusive item or two from a specialty catalog, which I then
never used.

What are your fatal distractions? Perhaps it's the hours you
lose to Facebook each day checking out friends' holiday plans;

the reality TV show that's more about elimination than elevation; the plastic debt you are piling up to buy "happiness"; or, when you stop by the tray of Christmas cookies just one more time at the office, you conveniently forget that your body is God's temple.

In the Christian calendar, Lent is the season of denial, when we begin to deal with the counterfeit dependencies we use as substitutes for the God life. This past Lent, for example, I decided to combat my materialism and ensure a right focus on God by giving up purchasing, with the exception of food and fuel.

To have a different kind of Christmas this year, let's practice a little Lenten spirit early. Let's repent of those areas or habits that keep Christ from being fully revealed in us and through us. Let's remove the fatal distractions. Let's reflect back to God—as best we can within our humanness—God's scandalous love.

Lord God, empower me to eliminate those false priorities and practices that are keeping me from experiencing, returning, and sharing your love with others this Christmas. Amen.

15. UNFAITHFUL

Then the Lord said to me, "Go and love your wife again, even
though she commits adultery with another lover. This will illustrate
that the Lord still loves Israel, even though the people have turned
to other gods and love to worship them." (Hosea 3:1 NLT)

I suppose the sad truth is that God is used to his people's inattention. The Old Testament is filled with accounts of God's people turning to other gods or lovers. Moses' brother Aaron crafted golden calves to appease the people during the desert exodus. Solomon built shrines to false gods in order to keep his many wives happy. King Ahab and Jezebel institutionalized the worship of Baal in all-out defiance of God.

You get the picture. The most repeated phrase in the book of Judges is "the children of Israel did evil in the sight of the Lord." That phrase describes the way generation after generation turned their backs on God to worship other gods—and this was right after Joshua had delivered them into God's land of promise! It's amazing that God made this covenantal relationship with his special people, the Israelites, and then continued to keep his end of the bargain despite the fact that they betrayed him time and time again.

One of the most powerful illustrations of God's scandalous love is found in the book of the obscure prophet Hosea. God directed Hosea, who represented God in the story, to marry a promiscuous woman named Gomer, who represented Israel.

God told Hosea not only to marry her, but to have children with her. The obedient Hosea married Gomer, and the inevitable happened. Gomer cheated, repeatedly, prostituting herself to the highest bidder. I imagine that Hosea must have looked carefully at each child Gomer bore, wondering which ones were his. Despite the many betrayals, God directed Hosea to return to Gomer and love her again, just as the Lord continued to love the unfaithful Israelites.

As Christians, we have also entered into a special covenant with God. Yet, like Gomer, we repeatedly stray. Sure, we may show up on Sunday morning playing the faithful spouse, but then we spend the rest of the week being, at best, indifferent to God. At worst, we start selling ourselves out to the false gods of gluttony, greed, and materialism as soon as we exit the church parking lot.

Through it all, God never stops pursuing us. Despite our unfaithfulness, each Christmas he sends his son as a tiny baby in humble and scandalous circumstances to gently buy us back.

Lord, thank you for loving me madly, passionately, and unconditionally despite my unfaithfulness. I recommit my life to you this Christmas. Amen.

16. TRUSTING THE PROMISE

*Mary said, "With all my heart I glorify the Lord! In the depths
of who I am I rejoice in God my savior. He has looked with favor
on the low status of his servant. Look! From now on, everyone will
consider me highly favored because the mighty one has done great
things for me. Holy is his name." (Luke 1:46-49 CEB)*

Mary, the mother of Jesus, perfectly modeled what it means
to have faith as defined in Hebrews: "Faith is the reality of what
we hope for, the proof of what we don't see" (Hebrews 11:1
CEB).

Mary was an unwed teenage mother of little economic
means. She lived in an intolerant culture that itself had long
suffered under the subjugation of a repressive Roman regime.
Despite the bleak nature of her outer circumstances, she clung
to hope and faith, singing God's praises and trusting God's
promises for the future. Mary believed in God's scandalous love
and knew that God would produce good out of what seemed to
be an impossibly bad situation.

Have you ever met someone like Mary, one of those people
whose presence and attitude make God more visible in the lives
of the people they touch?

David and May were members of Ginghamsburg Church.
Although they lived in Columbus, eighty miles away, they
attended worship each Saturday and then stayed until midnight,
serving with our teen outreach ministry. "D. J. Dave" staffed the

dance floor each weekend, spinning tunes and serving as a friendly, supportive ear for students. When the weekly drive became too much, David and May bought a small RV to park next to the youth building and slept there on Saturday nights.

David developed a persistent cough and was shocked to learn that he had terminal lung cancer—particularly upsetting since he had never smoked a day in his life. All who knew him were devastated. Despite his dire diagnosis, David exhibited remarkable faith. For as long as he was able, he continued to serve at the youth center, offering to students a powerful example of what it means to live with courage and trust in God. His message? No matter what happened, it was all good. He could lose his life, but he would never lose his faith.

Like Mary, David and his remarkable spirit have continued to inspire people even after his death. His story, captured on video, has demonstrated to thousands what it means to rely on and respond with gratitude to God's relentless love—no matter the circumstance.

Lord God, this Advent I will trust completely in your promises to bring good out of bad, to raise up the lowly, and to comfort the afflicted. Thank you, Lord, for your scandalous love. Amen.

17. FEARFULLY AND WONDERFULLY MADE

You are the one who created my innermost parts; you knit me
together while I was still in my mother's womb. I give thanks to
you that I was marvelously set apart.
(Psalm 139:13-14 CEB)

Last Christmas Eve, I was passing through a hallway at church and paused to say hello to Jack and Hannah, two thirty-something parents in our congregation. They had just finished snapping a picture of their two sons, and I commented that the boys looked almost like twins in their red Christmas vests and ties. Well, that wasn't completely accurate. The oldest son, Jamal, is a nineteen-year-old African American; the youngest is a toddler, white just like his mom and dad.

Jack and Hannah met Jamal through serving with our Clubhouse program, a teen-driven after-school tutoring program for kids from at-risk communities. In 2002 Jamal had started in the program, where he came to know Christ. When he was abandoned by his own family just before his senior year in high school, Hannah and Jack took him into their home and treated him as if he were their son. His own family may not have valued him, but Jack and Hannah, first as mentors and then as parental figures, saw something more. They and the Clubhouse participants would not let Jamal give up on himself. He was elected president of his high school senior class and is now attending American University in Washington, D.C. Jack and Hannah couldn't be more proud, always demonstrating a relentless love for Jamal.

It is easy for the father of lies to convince us that we have disappointed God, that we are not favored, and that God will never be with us. Don't listen. The Bible is filled with innumerable failures who went from zeros to heroes as they learned to live by faith and embrace God's grace, just as Jamal accepted the grace extended to him in his new family. Paul and Moses were murderers. Peter was a hothead. David was an adulterer and ordered a hit on his lover's husband. The list goes on. That's what God's scandalous love is all about. In spite of our failures and shortcomings, despite the condemnation of those around us, God always comes back to redeem us.

This Advent season, are you filled with doubt, fear, self-reproach, or perceived insignificance? Place this verse on the bathroom mirror and echo King David: "How precious to me are your thoughts, O God! How vast is the sum of them!" (Psalm 139:17 NIV).

Lord God, this Christmas I won't listen to the father of lies. I am a favored child of God, and you are always with me. Amen.

18. "I AM SENDING YOU"

All who are thirsty should come to me! All who believe in me should drink! As the scriptures said concerning me, "Rivers of living water will flow out from within him." (John 7:37-39 CEB)

Sometimes I think we confuse the second coming of Christ with the first. We jump right to the book of Revelation to see Christ return as the victorious King, judging the world and establishing a new heaven on Earth; and we forget that we are still living in the reality of the first coming, when God's Son came to Earth, not as victor, but as victim. He came as a baby thrust into the experience of the world's oppressed refugees. And, as Savior and suffering servant, Jesus continues to show up in the world's places of pain. We have a God who identifies with the slave chained in the hold of a ship, the Jewish prisoner in Auschwitz, the woman infected with HIV, and the orphan in the Darfur refugee camp.

We like to focus on the miracle of the resurrection. Frankly, resurrection is not a big deal for the God who created the universe. Jesus wasn't the first resurrection anyway; remember Lazarus, as well as a few others along the way? To me, the greatest miracle is not the resurrection, but the incarnation. That's scandalous love!

In light of all the atrocities in the world around us, many of us ask ourselves, "Where is God?" We often say, "Somebody ought to do something about that." Well, let me tell you: God has come down to do something about it, and you are the somebody he is doing it through! Jesus said, "As the Father sent me, so I am sending you" (John 20:21 CEB).

You may be thinking, "God surely doesn't mean me. What could I do? At best, it would only be a drop in the bucket." That's another great strategy of Satan. Evil tries to convince us that we are powerless, that we can't change anything. But Jesus says that we have full access to the unlimited resources of God, to "rivers of living water." As followers of Jesus, the word "can't" shouldn't be allowed in our vocabulary.

You have heard it said that the only thing necessary for evil to succeed is for good people to do nothing. It's true. We have been the recipients of God's scandalous love; now, go and actively live it out on behalf of others.

Lord, reveal to me today how you have designed, called, and equipped me to love others scandalously this Christmas. Amen.

WEEK FOUR

Jesus' Wish List

I can't say that I spent my entire life aware of Jesus' Christmas list—or caring, for that matter.

I was raised in a comfortably middle-class family. At Christmas, my sister and I would keep an eager eye out for the Sears Christmas catalog, then pore over the pages until they were dog-eared, circling our hoped-for treasures so that Mom (or Santa) would see them. Seems like the hot-ticket stocking stuffers in those days were items such as Slinkies, matchbox cars, Play Doh, and those crazy neon-haired troll dolls.

One year, my ultimate wish-list present was the infamous Red Ryder BB gun, memorialized in the movie, *A Christmas Story* (Metro-Goldwyn-Mayer, 1983). Over the years, my list became a bit more sophisticated, and expensive: LP albums, a Zenith transistor radio, a Schwinn ten-speed bike, and, by the time I reached my teens, a '68 Corvette Stingray. (For some reason, Santa never brought that one.) The older I got, the bigger the price tags became.

I still like to give and receive gifts. I love the way Carolyn's face lights up when I figure out just the right present for just the right occasion. I have great memories of my kids opening their presents on Christmas morning when they were small, and of opening my own when I was their age. However, the best Christmases we have ever experienced as a family have been those of the past eight or nine years, when we have intentionally focused on simplifying Christmas, choosing to celebrate our birthdays on our birthdays, and honoring Christ on his.

We still exchange simple gifts. Last year I was thrilled to get my daughter Kristen's new family photos on Christmas morning. My son Jonathan's striking photos of kids who have been served by our projects in the Sudan have been beautiful additions to our walls. Carolyn makes homemade granola for family, friends, and staff, and we encourage those who choose to gift us to contribute to the church's humanitarian relief projects on our behalf. Most importantly we have discovered, both in our family and in our Ginghamsburg Church family, the gift that makes Jesus smile on his birthday: our willingness to be his conduit, his resources, for blessing the world he loves.

This week, let's note the items on Jesus' Christmas wish list—and start checking them off.

19. THE PERFECT GIFT

*Then the king will reply to them, "I assure you that when you
have done it for one of the least of these brothers and sisters of
mine, you have done it for me." (Matthew 25:40 CEB)*

When we try to find the perfect gift for important people in our lives, Christmas can make us perfectly miserable.

Sometimes we worry about the perfect gift, because we love the people so much and don't want them to be disappointed. Other times, our stress has more to do with a desire to impress. Perhaps you try to outdo your co-worker Bill with the boss's gift this year, because you want that shot at an upcoming promotion. Yet at the same time, you don't want Bill to know that you are intentionally trying to one-up him, because he might look for his own opportunity to stab you in the back. What a dilemma! As parents, we show up outside the big-box electronics store in the middle of the night on Black Friday to be first in line for an over-marketed and under-available new gaming system. Because, if it isn't under the tree, the kid's year will simply be ruined. Meanwhile, commercials blasting over the airwaves ratchet up the pressure and potential for guilt. I could always make it a "December to remember" for my wife— if I were a millionaire!

Some people get worn out by "perfect present" stress and then simply give up. You know the types. Have you ever been re-gifted with somebody else's reject sweater from last year?

Have you received a Gucci handbag from a friend, only to realize when you examine it closely that the label spells it "Guccy?"

Fortunately, in Matthew 25, Jesus makes it very clear what he wants on his birthday. In fact, his "wish list" holds the same items we will be tested on for our final exam when we reach the Day of Judgment. I was hungry, and you gave me something to eat. I was thirsty, and you gave me a drink. I was in prison, and you visited me. I was naked, and you clothed me (Matthew 25:35). This is the simplest and clearest wish list you will ever receive, and perhaps the most challenging.

This Advent, let's worry more about gifting the Giver of all good things with what he wants for Christmas, and worry less about simply getting the goods.

Dear God, help me to love you by loving the least of these in real and tangible ways this Christmas. Amen.

20. WHAT'S IN YOUR HAND?

But if a person has material possessions and sees a brother or
sister in need and that person doesn't care—how can the love of
God remain in him? Little children, let's not love with words or
speech but with action and truth. (1 John 3:17-18 CEB)

The apostle John makes it clear that we are to use what we have to serve those in need, love the lost, and set the oppressed free. Words aren't enough; it takes action. Yet, many of us question how we are supposed to follow these directives when we seem to lack the gifts, talents, or resources.

You don't have to read very far into the Bible to find examples of people questioning how they are supposed to respond to God's call, when they don't seem to have what they need in order to do it. Moses is a classic example. In Exodus 3 and 4, God barely finished telling Moses to go back to Egypt to secure the release of God's people from four hundred years of slavery, before Moses began listing all the reasons why he was not the right guy, including the lack of ability and reputation to get the job done.

How did God respond to Moses' excuses? With a simple question: "What's that in your hand?" The item already in Moses' hand was a staff, a basic tool of a shepherd's trade. It was the same staff that later would evoke miracles in front of Pharaoh, part the Red Sea, bring water from a rock, and lead God's people to the edge of the Promised Land.

Do you feel that you don't have what it takes this year to give sacrificially toward Jesus' wish list? God asks the same question of you: "What is in your hand?" In the second year of our Christmas Miracle Offering at Ginghamsburg Church, many of our attendees took stock of what was in their hands, acknowledging what they already possessed and releasing it to God's purposes. Marta, a housecleaner, took on extra homes at night to feed people in Darfur. Jon sold an antique truck from his barn, using the proceeds to build a kindergarten for Sudanese children. Max, a ten-year-old, started running and took pledges from family and schoolyard pals for each mile he ran, to make sure at least one more child in Africa had access to clean water. A church cell group held a garage sale, no price tags attached, asking shoppers to give what they thought an item was worth; shoppers were told that the proceeds would go to serve a people who had been devastated by war, forgotten by the world, and were in dire need of compassion.

So, what's in your hand this Christmas?

Lord God, help me to release what I have so that your Kingdom can multiply. Amen.

21. A God of Both/And

*That evening his disciples came and said to him, "This is an
isolated place and it's getting late. Send the crowds away so they
can go into the villages and buy food for themselves." But Jesus
said to them, "There's no need to send them away. You give them
something to eat." (Matthew 14:15-16 CEB)*

In Matthew 14, we find Jesus and his disciples after a
tough day at the office, so to speak. A crowd of five thousand
had been following them around, hungry for the spiritual food
and healing that only Jesus could provide. Of course, people
being people, that spiritual hunger also turned into a very real
physical hunger, and the disciples found themselves with the
challenge of feeding the masses using only a few loaves of
bread and a couple of fish. Not concerned, Jesus took what
there was, blessed it, broke it . . . and no one went hungry. In
fact, there were leftovers!

Far too often we are limited in what we accomplish for
God because of a scarcity mentality. We forget that we serve
a God who has "cattle on a thousand hills" (Psalm 50:10
CEB). In 2 Kings 4, a widow cried out to the prophet Elisha,
saying that creditors were coming to enslave her sons. She
had no funds to repay the creditors, as the only possession of
any value at all in her home was one small jar of olive oil.
But, through God's miracle of multiplication and Elisha's in-
structions, that one small jar became a fortune's worth, limited

only by the number of jars the widow and her sons collected for filling. Elisha knew he served a God of abundance.

We also fall into the trap of an either/or mindset—the belief that we don't have enough to go around—versus the both/and mindset that reflects our limitless God. When Ginghamsburg Church first started investing in sustainable humanitarian projects in Darfur, Sudan, some well-meaning naysayers protested, pointing out that we have poverty in this country. Yes, we do, and shame on us. But we serve a God of abundance, a God who equips us to provide safe water, food, education, and hope to tens of thousands in the Sudan; in addition, he equips us to serve forty-thousand-plus people annually in Dayton, Ohio, our own backyard, through material assistance, jobs training, GED programs, and more. We don't serve a God who calls us to Dayton *or* Darfur, but a God who amply resources us for both Dayton *and* Darfur.

You are blessed! Where is God calling you to live and give abundantly this Christmas?

Lord, forgive me for limiting what I will do by limiting my thinking about what you can do. May I live with abundance this Advent. Amen.

22. GOOD NEWS FOR THE POOR

The LORD God's spirit is upon me, because the LORD has
anointed me. He has sent me to bring good news to the poor, to
bind up the brokenhearted, to proclaim release for captives, and
liberation for prisoners. (Isaiah 61:1 CEB)

In the early days of his ministry, Jesus stood in the pulpit of his hometown synagogue, reading these words from Isaiah as he boldly declared his mission statement. The gospel, his followers learned that day, is good news for the poor, oppressed, and marginalized. If it isn't for them, then it isn't the gospel. What a far cry this is from the so-called good news of Bigger, Better, and More that our consumerist culture proclaims from every television set, catalog, and mall, starting well in advance of each Christmas shopping season.

One of my staff members has two college-age sons. She recently noticed references to "first-world problems" on her sons' Facebook pages and those of their friends. First-world problems are frustrations or complaints that have meaning only to those of us who are privileged enough to live in wealthy countries. In fact, entire Web sites exist simply for people to list these first-world problems. Recent posts included: "I put a bandage on my thumb and now I can only text with one hand," and "It stinks having a check so large that I can't deposit it using my iPhone app." (Want to see more examples? Go to YouTube and type "first-world problems" in the search bar. Does the video take too long to load? There you go . . . another first world problem.)

At Christmas, we fail to see the physical poverty of the poor around us—those waiting for us to bring the good news of Immanuel—because we are too blinded by our own spiritual poverty. We have our own brokenness, a spiritual malaise that is a direct result of materialism. We are so focused on our first-world problems, we forget how Isaiah described us: the people of the Messianic kingdom. "They will rebuild the ancient ruins; they will restore formerly deserted places; they will renew ruined cities, places deserted in generations past" (Isaiah 61:4 CEB).

How will you bring good news to the poor this Christmas, and not just talk about it? It's time to go beyond simply hanging a new pair of two-dollar gloves on the mitten tree, or passing on a gently used toy for an adopted Christmas child. This Christmas, let's truly honor Jesus on his birthday.

Lord God, open my eyes to the poor and the brokenhearted. Help me to love them as you love them—and as you love me. Amen.

23. JUST, MERCIFUL, HUMBLE

*He has told you, O mortal, what is good. And what does the
Lord require of you? To act justly and to love mercy and to walk
humbly with your God. (Micah 6:8 NIV)*

Micah 6:8 provides a pretty good set of prerequisites for Jesus' wish list: To serve as Christ's hands, feet, and voice in the world, we must act with justice, love mercy, and walk humbly.

God calls us not simply to believe in justice, but to do justice. We have power with God through our actions toward other people, especially the poor and marginalized. Justice, a core biblical theme, is the very foundation of God's kingdom (Psalm 89:14). As followers of Jesus, we must always speak and act on behalf of those who lack a voice or influence. We must go where Jesus goes, do what Jesus does, and be who Jesus is.

To me, Brad is a living testimony to Micah 6:8. Brad is in his mid-sixties and is a successful business founder and owner. He has a beautiful home in a nearby community, as well as vacation homes in Hawaii and Colorado. Sounds like the American dream come true, doesn't it? Yet, Brad is also one of the humblest and most generous servants I know. Twice he has made the risky trip to the Sudan with our team, on his own dime, to encourage the people we are serving and to bring back stories of God's miracles to the Ginghamsburg family. He has also been a generous contributor to each year's miracle offering. When Brad is in town, you will typically find him teaching in the Backyard, our Sunday morning class for third through fifth graders. In fact, Brad may have the longest tenure of any servant on the Children's Ministry team. He's equally as loving and engaged with the kids we meet in Darfur; language is never a barrier with Brad. One of my favorite videos from our last trip to Sudan shows Brad enthusiastically leading Dinka children in the Ohio State cheer. O-H-I-O never looked so beautiful . . . or so much like Jesus. Brad is deeply blessed; and by blessing others, he continues to invest in the perfect gift for the Savior.

Most of us don't have two vacation homes; some of us don't own one home. But we do have a God who loves us, provides for us, and invites us to walk humbly with him this Christmas.

Lord, show me how to demonstrate your love, justice, and mercy on behalf of others this Advent. Amen.

24. SACRIFICE

He must increase and I must decrease. (John 3:30 CEB)

In John 3, Jesus' cousin, John the Baptist, was asked if he was jealous of Jesus' newly found fame. After all, people who would have flocked to John for baptism back in his prime were now seeking out Jesus instead. Wasn't John upset? John replied with a short sentence that I have used as a prayer mantra over the years: "More of you, Jesus; less of me." Here's an important corollary to that mantra: "More for you, Jesus; less for me." At Christmas we celebrate a Messiah who was born to die. Like Christ, we are called to give ourselves sacrificially for the world God loves. We are equipped to serve; we are blessed to bless; we are loved to love.

Each Christmas since 2004, we have challenged our Ginghamsburg congregation at Christmas to be more about Jesus, less about self. The people have responded faithfully year after year, whether in years of plenty or in years like 2008, when the final General Motors plant in the Dayton area closed its doors. That closure was another in a series of terrible economic blows to our largely blue-collar congregation. Each year, through good times and bad, God's people have found creative ways to change the world for Jesus.

Ginghamsburg is an ordinary place with ordinary people. The main campus is surrounded by soybean fields just below a small village and just above a struggling mid-sized city in the rust belt of Ohio. Those qualities make us a good example of how God uses ordinary people from ordinary places to accomplish extraordinary things. Although we have been blessed to invest nearly $6 million into the Sudan, it is still a pittance in comparison with what God could and would accomplish if every church and every follower of Jesus chose to live more simply so that others could simply live.

This year for Christmas, God wants you and everything about you, including your time, talent, and treasure. If you and your church were to choose one place of passionate mission and give sacrificially to it through your works and wealth, how might the world look different by next Advent season? If you already have that place of mission, how will you take it to the next level, giving Jesus a birthday party he will never forget?

Jesus is waiting for your answer.

Lord, I will celebrate your birthday this Christmas. Fill me with your Spirit, mold me in your likeness, and use me for your purpose. Amen.

WEEK FIVE

By a Different Road

One of the professions most maligned in our culture for not having a strong moral compass is the stereotypical "used car salesman." You know the type I'm talking about—fast-talking, eager to sell anything that moves, and enthusiastically stating that the previous owner was the proverbial little old lady who only drove the car to church on Sundays. At Ginghamsburg, we are blessed to have many people in the car business who are the antithesis of the stereotype. These are folks who demonstrate what it means to be attentive to God's voice and then are willing to take a different road, making the unexpected choice, on behalf of the Kingdom—just as the Magi did over two thousand years ago.

Jack, Mike, and Sam are three auto dealership owners in our church family. They are incredible servant leaders and generous givers to each year's miracle offering on behalf of our sisters and brothers in the Sudan. Jack is always willing to loan out vans for our big events, Mike has led multiple teams to the

Gulf for Hurricane Katrina relief, and Sam has traveled to Darfur with me and made significant investments of time and resources to be on mission in Jamaica, Cuba, and Vietnam. Sam's trips have been featured, at our request, in some of our mission worship videos, since his enthusiasm for missions is contagious. But what I most appreciate about Jim is the quiet service he does behind the scenes, without fanfare or recognition.

Chris, one of my staff members, recently told me that he had driven Sarah, a single mother, to Sam's dealership. Previously a stay-at-home mom, Sarah was reeling from a bad divorce and a vindictive ex-husband, who, without her knowledge, had accumulated significant debt. Her car, acquired in the divorce settlement and her only form of transportation to work, had been repossessed. Sarah arrived at Sam's lot with $4000 to spend—money from a brother's loan and the church's love fund. Sam had a 2001 Ford Taurus on the lot with 200,000 miles on it that her cash would cover outright. But, a few moments later he put her into a 2003 Buick Rendezvous, a $10,500 value instead with only 80,000 miles, which was a better, safer fit for her young family. Sam ate the difference in cost—quietly, quickly, and compassionately. He is an inspiring witness to me in word and deed, daily demonstrating what it means to be part of a countercultural movement.

This week, like Sam, let's travel "by a different road."

25. CONVERSION

They entered the house and saw the child with Mary his mother. Falling to their knees, they honored him. Then they opened their treasure chests and presented him with gifts of gold, frankincense, and myrrh. Because they were warned in a dream not to return to Herod, they went back to their own country by another route. (Matthew 2:11-12 CEB)

Last New Year's Eve, I asked my Facebook friends, "What are your 'God' or spiritual growth resolutions for the coming year?" One friend replied, "I need to lose twenty-five pounds by taking care of the temple of God." Another declared, "I plan to spend more time in God's Word, not just getting through the reading but meeting God in the reading." A third planned to "pay off debt to be a better example to my children." Several resolutions dealt with unloading or downsizing unwanted stuff.

Of course, as we soon discover, the problem with resolutions is that good intentions don't necessarily equate to desired results. I have always believed there is one new birth in a person's life, but there can be many conversions. A conversion, more than just the intention to act, is the moment of commitment, the point of no return. It's the definitive point in time when a declaration is made to do God's will in an area of inconsistency or neglect.

Even though I had a new birth in Christ in 1969, my conversion to practice a consistent daily time of devotion through Bible reading, prayer, and journaling didn't occur until August

1994. In June 1992, I made the disciplined commitment to start my marriage over. My commitment to tithe became real in May 1976. I finally started getting my physical life together through healthy eating and exercise in September 2000. I know first-hand that changing old life actions and attitudes is difficult. It takes far more than a resolution; it takes repentance. It requires, like the Magi, being attentive to God's voice and then being willing to travel by a different road home.

What old life practices is Jesus calling you to discard this Christmas as you celebrate the incarnation and prepare for the New Year? In what areas of your life are you procrastinating? In what ways are you failing to deal with bad habits or to begin healthy new ones so that your life reflects the excellence of God? Where do you need to repent, respond to God's voice, and reorient?

Lord, help me to identify the places where my life does not reflect your excellence and then have the courage and commitment to travel by a different road. Amen.

26. RIGHT-SIZING YOUR LIFE

Stop collecting treasures for your own benefit on earth, where
moth and rust eat them and where thieves break in and steal them.
Instead, collect treasures for yourselves in heaven, where moth and
rust don't eat them and where thieves don't break in and steal
them. Where your treasure is, there your heart will be also.
(Matthew 6:19-21 CEB)

Jesus came to Earth to proclaim that the kingdom of God is near. So, what does this kingdom look like? It is the place where God's invisible rule and activity are made visible. It is the physical representation of heaven on earth, demonstrated through a community of people living in submission to God's authority—a community that puts the resources of heaven into operation.

When we acknowledge Jesus as Lord, it means he begins to define everything about our lives, including what we do with our money. But, we struggle, because God's kingdom values are upside down from the world's values. For most of us, the primary value is financial security. That is, we don't get up in the morning with the intention of pursuing the kingdom of God; instead we go to work to earn money, pay bills, buy Christmas presents, and maybe, just maybe, save a little along the way. But Jesus said that when we make the kingdom our number-one priority, we go beyond fiscal abundance to life abundance. God will take care of our needs as we "desire first and foremost God's kingdom" (Matthew 6:33). Why did Jesus talk more about money than any other subject including prayer or faith? Because, your money is your demonstration of what you truly value . . . and whom you really trust.

You have read about Ginghamsburg's investment toward saving lives in the Sudan. You may be thinking, "That's great, but my church doesn't have thousands of people in it." I hear that. But I also know that when we seek first God's kingdom, trust in his hand, and remember that we are the only bank accounts God has, miracles can happen. I came to Ginghamsburg in 1979, and my first "growth movement" was when a congregation of about ninety people dropped to sixty. At Christmas 1981, Ethiopia was experiencing a severe famine. Our whole church budget was $32,000 a year. But, when we remembered that "Christmas is not our birthday" and challenged ourselves to bring for Ethiopia an amount equal to what we had spent on our families, seventy people brought a total of $18,000.

I speak from firsthand experience: Church size doesn't matter; kingdom focus does. Challenge your faith community to commit to a different road this Christmas.

God, thank you for the abundance in my life. Help me encourage my faith family this Christmas to act sacrificially on behalf of others. In Jesus' name, Amen.

27. Proactive Parenting

*But be on guard and watch yourselves closely so that you
don't forget the things your eyes saw and so they never leave your
mind as long as you live. Teach them to your children and your
grandchildren. (Deuteronomy 4:9 CEB)*

In God's world, *parent* is not synonymous with *best
friend,* though many of us confuse the two. In our me-focused
culture, with its slippery moral slope, parenting is increasingly
important. A key practice for reorienting your life in the New
Year is to commit to proactive parenting. Even if you aren't a
biological parent, you are to be a spiritual parent and mentor
to younger generations.

Proactive parenting isn't always fun. My son Jonathan is
the athlete I wanted to be but wasn't. In high school, he
played football, basketball, and baseball. During his freshman
year, our youth group was going to Jamaica on a mission trip.
It was important to Carolyn and me as his biological and
spiritual parents to ensure that he went, and he did; but that
trip caused Jonathan to sit on the bench for his next three basketball games—not an easy thing to do for someone with his
competitive spirit. When Jonathan played baseball at the University of Pennsylvania, he attended Catholic Mass when
other options weren't feasible because of games. We aren't
Catholic, but we had always taught our children that it's not

about us—it's about God. Today, both of our children and their spouses are followers of Jesus and are serving the kingdom.

Joseph and Mary were proactive parents. After Jesus' birth, they brought him to Jerusalem to present him to the Lord. Then, "when Mary and Joseph had completed everything required by the Law of the Lord, they returned to their hometown, Nazareth in Galilee" (Luke 2:39). In your Bible, circle the word "everything." Mary and Joseph didn't do just the easy stuff; they did everything that God's word required of parents. Under their care, Jesus "grew up and became strong. He was filled with wisdom, and God's favor was on him" (Luke 2:40 CEB).

Their vigilance didn't end with Jesus' infancy. Each year, Jesus' parents took him to the Passover festival in Jerusalem, not an easy journey. "When he was twelve years old, they went up to Jerusalem according to their custom" (Luke 2:42 CEB). In Greek, the word for custom means "habit." On this trip, Jesus' parents were dismayed to find him missing in action a full day into their return journey home. They scurried back to Jerusalem to find him still at church. Clearly, Jesus had internalized the priorities and passions of his parents.

This Christmas, what are your priorities toward your biological and spiritual children?

Lord, help me to show my children how to be sources of blessing to others rather than self-focused consumers of stuff. Amen.

28. SERVING

*Let your light shine before people, so they can see the good
things you do and praise your Father who is in heaven.
(Matthew 5:16 CEB)*

Jesus says, in John 3:17, "God didn't send his Son into the world to judge the world, but that the world might be saved through him." God sent Immanuel to raise up a community of disciple priests who would be committed to changing the world through God's power. Right before Jesus' ascension into heaven he said, "You will receive power when the Holy Spirit has come upon you, and you will be my witnesses in Jerusalem, in all Judea and Samaria, and to the end of the earth" (Acts 1:8 CEB).

Too many times, Christians limit the meaning of witness to words—telling people about Jesus. But when the Bible describes witness it goes far beyond words to include the content of our character and our actions. We are the salt of the earth. We are the light of the world. We are to become a community of disciples and priests, the living demonstration on earth of God's presence, character, and purpose.

I was raised in a household where I was forced to go to church, Sunday school, and Bible school. I hated it then, although I regularly thank my mom now for making me go. But here is the problem: I found church boring and irrelevant, and many people I saw there were judgmental and hypocritical. Worse than that, in the 1960s they were racist. On one hand they taught me in Sunday school that Jesus loves all the children of the world, and on the other hand they used hate-filled language to criticize Dr. Martin Luther King, Jr., and the civil rights movement. How conveniently we forget that we must be the gospel before anyone else is going to *believe* the gospel.

Ask the Spirit to reveal to you in your prayer time today where your life actions are not matching your faith words. Next, identify practical steps you can take right now, this week, to be Christ's light in the world. Will you pull up an extra chair at the Christmas table for a neighbor with no place to go? Will you lead the members of your small group—or, better yet, your kids—in serving at the homeless shelter? Will you give more generously than you had planned to your church's mission programs?

Remember, miracles begin with simple acts that honor Jesus on his birthday.

Dear Lord, let me be your light, a witness to your love for others in both word and deed. Amen.

29. WITNESS

"We have found the Messiah." (Andrew to his brother Peter in John 1:41 CEB)

Faith requires right belief and right action. But we also need to name the name and tell others the good news about Jesus, not just do good deeds.

As a young Christian with Campus Crusade, witnessing was one of the most difficult things I had to do. The popular way at the time was to walk up to people on the street, gospel tract in hand, and start the conversation like this: "Do you know where you would go if you were to die tonight?" Brian, a fellow Campus Crusade volunteer, would follow me around, cheering me on, until I would make myself do it. That approach isn't what I would recommend today, but at the time it shocked me how the Holy Spirit prepared some people to hear the message in spite of my awkwardness. I learned from that experience that all we can do is witness by the power of the Spirit, and leave the results to God.

Lost people matter, and it amazes me how God chases us down. In 1968 I was in a rock group, and when two band members were busted with drugs, my music career came to an end. For the next few months it seemed that everywhere I turned, some Jesus freak was waiting for me. It was so irritating. I would be as rude as possible, and all they would do in return was show love. I even thought I could escape God by getting out of town, so I headed south and wound up in Arkansas. One day I found myself in a men's room at a little two-pump gas station in Arkansas, and what was written on the wall? "Jesus saves all who want him." It bothered me so much that I told my girlfriend about it when I got back home. Within two years, maybe in part because of those messages, I quit running from the radical love of God—a God who hugs prodigals and sends his Son to redeem them, no matter the cost.

The best way to witness is not to shove Jesus down anyone's throat, but to show (good deeds) and then tell (the reason). The first part of Ginghamsburg's mission statement reads, "Bring seeking people into a life celebration with Jesus." That word, "seeking," is crucial; beating someone about the head and shoulders with your Bible is not going to do it. Leave the convincing up to the Holy Spirit. But, remember, friends don't let friends stay lost from God.

Whom are you building a relationship with that doesn't know Jesus Christ? Whom are you serving? Whom are you inviting to join the party this Christmas?

Lord, make my witness powerful and effective. Give me your heart for the lost. Amen.

30. DAILY BREAD

People don't live on bread alone. No, they live based on
whatever the LORD says. (Deuteronomy 8:3 CEB)

Seven years ago, when my parents moved into a senior adult community, I received the expected phone call from my mom that I needed to go into their basement to sort through boxes of stuff belonging to me that had accumulated through the years. What an experience! One of the first items I uncovered was my Lionel Train Set. I couldn't resist spending the next hour trying to set it up and make the engine run. It didn't work. The tracks were rusty from fifty years of moisture in the basement, and the motor was frozen. It's amazing how the gifts we anticipated so eagerly through the years become little more than rust and dust collectors. Christmas should be about so much more!

About seven hundred years before Christ was born, Micah prophesied that the Messiah would be born in Bethlehem, which means "House of Bread" in Hebrew and "House of Flesh" in Arabic. Years later, Jesus said, "People won't live only by bread, but by every word spoken by God" (Matthew 4:4 CEB). Actually, Moses was the first to teach this, in Deuteronomy 8, fourteen hundred years before Jesus showed up. During forty years in the wilderness, God's chosen people had to depend on daily bread from heaven for their sustenance. Luke was delivering the same message when he described the place where Mary put Jesus for the first few hours after birth. It was a manger—a feeding trough hewn out of rock where God's creatures could come and eat to sustain life.

I get distracted easily, especially at Christmas, and I start seeking life, my daily bread, from non-life-giving sources. Sometimes I can spend more time preparing for Christmas than preparing for Jesus. They are not the same thing! We first need to receive the real gift, which is never a present under the tree but the presence of God in Jesus Christ.

But it's not enough to receive the gift. We are to *be* the gift. Jesus comes into the world through our lives. We were created, in other words, to be God's feeding trough. It's only then that we will experience a different kind of Christmas, and the joy of living and giving like Jesus.

Lord Jesus, come into every dimension of my being. Invade my thoughts. Be my priority. Not my way, Lord, not my will, but yours. Use me for the purpose for which you made me this Christmas, and in every day of my life to come. Happy Birthday! Amen.